The Book of Festus

The Book of Festus

John Wall Barger

Copyright © 2015 John Wall Barger
All rights reserved

Palimpsest Press
1171 Eastlawn Ave.
Windsor, Ontario. N8S 3J1
www.palimpsestpress.ca

Book and cover design by Dawn Kresan. Typeset in Adobe Garamond Pro and Edwardian Script, and printed offset on Rolland Zephyr Laid at Coach House Printing in Ontario, Canada. Edited by Jim Johnstone.

Palimpsest Press would like to thank the Canada Council for the Arts, and the Ontario Arts Council for their support of our publishing program. We also acknowledge the assistance of the Government of Ontario through the Ontario Book Publishing Tax Credit.

Library and Archives Canada Cataloguing in Publication

Barger, John Wall, 1969–, author
    The book of festus / John Wall Barger.

Poems.
ISBN 978-1-926794-23-5 (pbk.)

    I. Title.

PS8603.A734B66 2015   C811'.6   C2014-907660-6

Contents

Invocation /11

I. THE BRIDGE

His Splendiferous Bicycle /19
Diorama of Spangled Bike, at Harbour /20
Eric the Red Cat /21
House of the Deaf Man /22
The Feast /25
Dream Map /27
The Kissing Bridge (Dismantled, 1861) /29
Sees the Deaf Man, /30
Smiths' Fields /31
The Junk Room /32
Patronymics of His Bike *(The Flying Haligonian)* /33
Adios, Deaf Man /36
Showdown with a Bone Ghost at The Nothing's O.K. Corral /37
Sallying Forth /39
The Covered Way /41

II. THE AXE

Haligonians, to Festus /45
Holy Cross Cemetery /47
Festus Maximus, To Himself /48
Off-Course, Citadel Hill, the Bone Ghost Sings of Electricity /49
Map Song N° 1 /50
The White Well, 1861 /51

The Girding of Spring Garden Road /53
Park Lane Mall, An Introduction /54
Festus Engages Spring Garden Road in Dialogue /56
Hermit Crab at Park Lane Aquarium /57
Map, in Electric Light /59
Down /60
Open Curtains /62
Sally Gone /72
Public Gardens, 1761 /73
Byplay /74
By-Ground Sally /75
Oxen, Sun /76
Map Song N° 2 /77
Ceremony—Eating in Front of TV /78
What Park Lane Thinks, Stomping Public Gardens /79
In Memoriam, Sally /80

III. THE COW

Festus, Hansel & Grendel /85
Were There Testimonials? /89
Map Song N° 3 /90
The Egg Pond /91
Park Lane Approacheth /92
Humungous Bos Taurus! /93
Bullfight /94
Showdown with Park Lane the Crayfish /95
Ceremony—Diving into a Good Movie /96
Festus, The Movie /98

What Manner of Film Was This?   /99
What Lay at the Poem's Feet   /101
Matronymics of the Girl   /102
Showdown   /103
Where You Been? Asks the River   /106

Acknowledgements   /109
Author Biography   /110

Invocation

Festus, having forgot,
woke, citizen in the City of himself.
Festus was nothing,
was shell, animalcule, glacial drift.
Ages on ages roll'd over Festus.
Festus uncurl'd to peninsula.
Festus Freshwater River sang the length of City.
Festus wolfpack howl'd.
General Festus Eyre Massey
wolf'd Mi'kmaq. Pioneer Festus
buried his own hatchet-heart,
construct'd the Angus Festus Macdonald Bridge,
curs'd himself & then forgot.
Festus cover'd Freshwater River with concrete
& raz'd the Kissing Bridge that forded it.
And then forgot.
Festus butcher'd & ate every cow of every colonist,
crow'd the eyes of human dead,
pour'd a checkerboard of concrete streets
over the clamorous gods
& then forgot,
& then forgot,
waking, citizen in the City of Halifax,
City of himself.

Woke each morning & forgot.
Dream, garbage, childhood, keys, Sally.

Forgot all he had forgot.

Forgetting!—What? All, *all.*
Riding bicycle, meeting
young girl, laying claim to journey.

Long ago, unblinking, awestruck,
Festus was eye, a pool
reflecting sky, no space between
eye & sky but a vision
of wolfish clouds, birds, moon,
stars, dice flung by gods,
their grace of rotation
a song in that eye

which a snail climbs over
& down his nose, into his throat,
singing, sinking
into memory of sound, river
of sound. River!
Ah, eye of Festus, throat
of Festus, time a dream
of song … Then torso curls
to peninsula, then feet
curl into rhizome
of stone, then snail curls
under tongue, then throat curls
shut, then eye
closes. Festus wakes,
citizen in the City
of self, alone under the sky.

Across a dream of words
he walks, gathering words
—so fragile, hard to hold,
each like a rolling paper
on fire—from sidewalks, trees,
pocketing, carefully, all.

Upon the word *sidewalk*,
under the word *sky*
he shuts his eyes,
smells the word *seaweed*,
inhales deeply
the word *oxygen*;
on this April day
upon the word *pier*
beside the word *harbour*,
having misplaced
a dear word: *bicycle*.

Check pockets, Festus.
Find your word.
Walk across *Halifax*,
ear to *concrete*.
Dig in *soil*.
Do you hear, faintly, your word?
No?

Then he hears—*river*.
He whispers, *river*,
lies on his back,

river,
river,
heart a page in an old man's fist,
body a body
in ancient watercourse, this
passage …

A bird flies past, overheard,

articulation of
              bird   *bridd*
                                brydde
                                          bryd
                                                    brygg

The word birrs, whirrs,
ungirds.

Something is remembering me.

I. THE BRIDGE

His Splendiferous Bicycle

Ecce Festus Minimus
forgot it,
unlocked on the grass, other end of town.

Rheofestus. Torrent of Festus!
What'll ye do?

Is it purloined? he mumbles.

No, not as yet.

Though a small girl with a gun dog
traces her finger
along its crescent seat
under a banana moon.

Brother, you can almost feel it
down your spine.
The dusk unriveted.

Diorama of Spangled Bike, at Harbour

Waves. Dark-skinned, lambent as Faust's
Leather socks, a girl in her closet

With speculum. Carbon, charred oil.
Gas stations used to smell this way.

How'd I get here? questions Festus.
A maple leaf on a flag

Flaps, as if to say,
Your way, O Festus, is hallowed.

Or was it *hollowed?* Closing his eyes
Dartmouth glitters like peags on a spoke.

Eric the Red Cat

feeds feeds from a blue bowl on deck of an ex-navy
gravy boat—CSS Acadia,

now stripped bare for tourists—
& regards F. on the wharf.

Festus, to Halifax: "Wyche maryneer
impregnat'd bye a skoole-gurle

layd thee, Egge?"
Wails he, "Mayst I ne'er haf domynyon

o'er fysches fowles beestes
ore anye cryature crepyng on th' earthe," &c.

—When Eric pads down the plank
& purrs,

"Oh you will you will despite yourself."

House of the Deaf Man

Festering, hands on head,
he tries to recall
why he went out of the house
to sit by the sea

without his bicycle!

Miaou! Eric the Red Cat
saunters past him
off pier to an anchor (Festus
follows), hop-

skips the wood shell playground boat,
curls up on paintcaked boots
of an old man leaning
on cane in fog.

I, Festus, impressed,
puff a perfecto,
climb the low bow
for a quaff

—Ah, tacit man!
truculent in spattered coveralls,
limping offpath over train-
yard, gravel lot, a hovel
at the mouth of Barrington
the Deaf Man enters.

Turpentine, vinegar wine.
Someone gouged walls
with paint, a clenched hand.
Upon broken planks & wall-
paper, a murderous mural
in oils like double shotgun blasts—

> Humus, moraine, shell, wolfpack, moon.
> Tipis, giants, ravens, stars, forest, silence.
> A skylarge canoe floats downharbour
> crammed with sailors, facetwisted sea dogs,
> fire-hair'd bawds, dwarves, prisoners,
> oleaginous ogres, deviant satyrs, ghosts
> o' bones! The Ancient of Days among
> whispers verities, palms uplifted, as
> *holy fuck* a hunchback with a glistening cock
> slits his throat. O bo'sun, what sails!
> Ships, black! Ships, hollow! How elegant
> & tall, your slave ships! Tall men, privateers
> infernal, bloodcrusted masters of these
> our gridwork streets, belt out b'ys yar
> soul-shudd'ring shanty, *Raised in Rock-*
> *head*, sings a wretch gibbeted on a cross …
> *Died in the poorhouse*, sings a flogged
> man in the workhouse … *Halifax,*
> *Halifax!* sing the orphans, *Go to Hell-ifax!*
> Men on spoons, men bagpipin', fiddlin',
> swillin' grog, jug rum—Ah! House
> of mercy—wickedeyedwhoremother,

spreadeagled Methodist! House of grace!
I'll give ya 30 pieces o' silver for tha'
dribblin' Injun scalp, wait b'y put it on
yar head *lah-di-dah* now by da lard dy'n
yar a washerwoman a feather'd bride
a newborn aslippin' astumblin' placenta-
slick headlong out of the canoe lickin'
yar lips spittin' & hissin' at a naked
Jamaican Maroon chain'd to the paddle.

And here is *he*—
the deaf artist in the flesh
smiling warmly beside this his portrait;
lurid gaps 'tween sepia teeth,
wet paintbrush gripped
'tween index finger & thumb.

Festus—"Ahem! Greetings,
wise sir, good Master Painter.
I, suburb-born ... shall, um,
desire you of more acquaintance ..."

Tea steams between.

The Feast

Deaf Man has made strong tea
in a tin pot, sits beside F.
at a Formica table
    before a *photograph*:
two long-hair'd whooping cranes
above a bigeyed boy in OshKosh B'goshes
leaning on a yellow bicycle,
between father's animal smile
& mother's open gaze.
      Deaf Man plants
a yellow fingernail
on the image of the boy:
Festus shrugs.
    A big rat gnaws crusts
on the counter. Festus
puts hand over heart as thanks
but the good host (grey beard,
mane unbrushed, shirt paint-soaked,
fingers long, feet bare, toenails
busted) waves it off.
     Among men
     nothing said.
Festus nods off.
Deaf Man grins, leads the inchoate
up dark & narrow stairs
to a little room,
a rough cot in the corner.
Victorian wallpaper
peels with asphodels.
     Alone,

Festus reads a newspaper,
doodling on it
with a lump of coal:
he draws a bicycle & *?*
& asks aloud, *What is at stake?*
He sleeps, dreams
                fog; an impregnable castle—
fortress of a Rat King: Festus walks
its ramparts, touches the cool thick stones:
beyond the black door is a feast.
Irresistible! But he doesn't knock.
Why not?

Dream Map

Festus wakes. His drawing has changed.
The bike doodle, reworked,

nimble strokes
in the hand of his host:

a headline (*Cole Harbour High
Racism Boils*),

wet with India ink,
invokes the familiar banana seat,

fat back tire, slim front,
& the majestic arch of handlebars.

The bike—charmed—shapeshifts
on the page: the tires turn

& turn! Before his eyes
it morphs to topography: forest, streets.

Harbour the potbelly of a City.
Why, it's *Halifax!*

Sure enough: there be two bridges,
a Star-of-David Citadel.

X marks the present spot: dead centre
of the spinning Back Wheel.

At the bull's eye
of the Front Wheel: the Commons.

The land between
linked with a blood-red line. Water, *river.*

"E'en so"—Festus nibbles his nail,
the auroral City surging over its sleepers—

"no river runs through Halifax."

The Kissing Bridge (Dismantled, 1861)

What glistens this way, O City?
Motherload railroads, tracked
where the Kissing Bridge stood.

Wait! What bridged?

A culverted cavity
underneath
where men shoot up.

Favoured haunt. Drenched embrace.
Where's *my* heroine?
Where—

(when *damn!* upon this bridge
a greeneyed lass
kisses my cheek,
I drop my perfecto
in the river)

—the new path across?
Erased, O Festus! Like a map drawn in pencil.

Sees the Deaf Man,

with his eyes, the head of the sacrificial horse which is the City—
its gaping mouth, the fog of its breath, its back,
abdomen, underbelly, flanks, ribs, stomach.
When the horse yawns, the Deaf Man sniffs, sniffs, drags
his big potholed nose on the wall—& *hears* with his harkening body
the hydraulic displacement beneath his house,
under streets, blood greasy & corrosive pumped
through sewers & glottal caverns, as if the City itself
had placed its fingers in its ears
                                      to listen to its own heart beating.

Smiths' Fields

Where sat the noxious tanneries,
           where crawls the City
on its belly,
      where yawns the trainyard on the sea.
                                  O industry—
halitosis! Denizens hold their noses.
Poplars of Point Pleasant Park dance side by side
on a hill, modestly.

       1881—
Here Schmidt, renowned *Scheißkopf,* soaked
deerskin in urine, scraped hairs with a straightrazor
gulping a smeared carafe, schnapps,

cooling his hammer in Freshwater River.

His brother found him head
over heels in the hearth
beside their solution of animal brains.

A violent flow. Headwaters.

Morning.
Festus takes a Kirk-Douglas-as-*Spartacus* breath—
TV atumbles off flatbed truck

headlong,
Schmidt *on-screen* mouthing
                      Du! Ja, du, Festus!
                      Upriver. Go, boy—or ye deserve yar foul end.

The Junk Room

Festus, frogophile,
lived in a house on a hill
as a boy

in a room without sisters,
brothers, windows—
just soldiers, yo-yos, a troll doll,

—connected by a sealed door
to a room
painted black:

jars of laughing monkeys
linking arms, a circular saw, a mirror,
large unbeautiful things,

where poor Ahab the Orange, King of the Afghan,
crawled to die
under the skeleton of a military bunk.

—I, Festus, beyond the door,
push Tonka trucks,
wake with deep impressions on my cheek.

Patronymics of His Bike *(The Flying Haligonian)*

Yellow!

One hesitates to name,
yet—
    1970 Schwinn Lemon Peeler

        (ye be wise withal
        to admit it more
        silence than this)

—Behold!

> *In the seventh year of Stacey, king of Duncan Street,*
> *Bobby, brother of Richie, reigned for a week*
> *at Oxford School, his arrogance spiralling like sand*
> *o'er the desert spoils & trash of the schoolyard.*
> *Now the people were camped against Duncan Street;*
> *they spake, "Stacey has conspired to steal Bobby's bike."*
> *It so happened that this bicycle had always been Stacey's,*
> *so this year—the fourth of Festus leaf-raker,*
> *only child—Stacey declared war on Bobby & Richie,*
> *trying to steal his own bike back while they supped.*
> *Their father, seizing Stacey, spake, "Because of the sins*
> *which you have sinned, doing evil in sight of the TV,*
> *bullying tiny Festus, bellyacher, who doesn't know*
> *any fuckin' better, & in your sin, which you did,*
> *made all Halifax sin, therefore I bequeath your bike*
> *to Festus lawn-mower, when he comes of age,*
> *to preserve his luminosity, always." Now the rest*
> *of the acts of Stacey & his conspiracy which he*

carried out, are they not written in The Book of Festus
of the Kings & Queens of Halifax?

Since 1970,
Byron, immaculate first owner;
After Byron, his brother Darren;
After Darren, Colin (filched from Dominion parking lot!)

After which passed seven dank years in a garage

After Colin, Stacey;
After Stacey, Bobby;
After Bobby, his brother Richie;
After Richie, Festus (at 12)

                                              Downhill!
Beside the Citadel on Duke Street hoping the red light will change
will change will change

Does nature, its broken hummingbirds or bees,
contain a *dearth*, in any form, as poignant
as that of Festus, so far from his bicycle?

From what dark soil was this spectre called forth?

From the rich earth
below Santa Cruz, California
was the Flying Haligonian
called thence to be assembled
in the Land of China
during the late Mao dynasty.

Will your idiot genealogist attain his *Sangraal*?

    Rest assured, O sluggards, white slaves.
    Cast your bread!
    Drink your wine!

    At the end of his journey
    Festus will find his yellow bicycle
    where it lies
            openly
                    under the moon.

Adios, Deaf Man

Door of Deaf Man: *bang* locked
blinds drawn. F. taps window, circles house.
Locked!
He hollers for benefactor.

Through slot, Deaf Man is viewed
painting Festus into the awful canoe
of satyrs & sailors, the malodorous mural.

Blinds are drawn.

    But why, shouts F. pitiably, *am I afraid of the sea?*

There—
the map at his feet.
    No longer of Halifax, or bicycle

        but
            sun! dusk sun, a skull,
            sun skull, grinning,
            malignant, a dream
            of bones, reeking oils
            —what hand drew this?

                The map moves.

Bones of the sky?
    He puts in pocket.

Showdown with a Bone Ghost at The Nothing's O.K. Corral

Your heart is a tactic whispered by soldiers,
slurs a voice in the culvert.

Midday sun.

Into gloom Festus peers: piss, cig butts, graffiti twists & tags.
No occupants.

A strategy shared on the battlefield.
                                        —"*My* heart?"

A giggling goblin
ruptures the light
red eyes like halogen lamps
nose a broken pedal
collagen obtruding cheek-skin
like teeth of a sprocket
                        vice-grips our hero
with an ashen hand, a *grave hand*,
bones spearing out;
                on the other palm
a television.
Tiny screen, frenzy
of green, x-rays:

> *Bicycle in grass,*
> *little girl singing*
> *beside a man*
> *drowned in a river*

Festus shakes loose, comes face to hand with another scene:

> *A crayfish in a glass tank*
> *hooks a claw over the rim*
> *falls on tiles clambers*
> *cockeyed like a crystal*
> *tank click clank past*
> *toilet kitchen junk room*
> *& halts in a doorway ...*

"Mom!" shrieks a boy,

        "The fish is here—
he's got his clickers up!"
                    Static.

Sallying Forth

Festus—hand on throat, gasping
—watches his own face in the TV hand
say:
> *Hear me, Festus.*
> *We are storm-tossed,*
> *afflicted; surely we have*
> *been kind to Halifax,*
> *have climbed the summit*
> *of the Citadel, peered down*
> *upon the sleepers,*
> *this wilderness like a City*
> *uninhabited; weary*
> *of holding the stories*
> *shut away in our bones.*
> *O land, land, land ...*

F.—But Mr. Bone Ghost, when did I say that?

The ghoul—hand squawking
unintelligibly—lurches at
the bright map in F.'s pocket.
"Where ya get *that*?!"

"It's a map to my bike."

"Idjit! It's a river map!
Gimmie!" He strains, anguished;
his hide in view of sun & power wires
sizzles—
> "Your *skin*, Mr. Jack-o'-lantern."

"Halfwit," he spits. "Electricity is poison!"
& hobbles off, spaugfoot.
Festus follows, uphill.

Inglis Street, why do you reek
of cabbage & calamity,
as if the Devil had thrown open his doors
for them
& these barrel-chested houses
to crumble into?

The Covered Way

When
Freshwater River was buried

here at Green Street
once a bridge

a bridge traversed
this parking lot.

Then Sobeys
was erected, 1966.

Yet no plaque, tourist centre, or clairvoyant
to recall the decree—

> *Citadel opened to assault from Covered Way;*
> *heavily treed ravine to be razed* ... (Gen. E. Massey, 1777)

Red river, wine river, my heart was once,
from which all water flowed

into which Haligonians leapt, tall hats flying off
ecstatically.

II. THE AXE

Haligonians, to Festus

And the people cried out,

You have rejected us!
You have broken us!
You have show'd the Mall
how to breastfeed from us!
Have murdered our cows!
Made the land quake!

Was it you that raged against rivers?
Was it your rage that stopped the flow of waters?

For now the river is an old boot
For now the river is lung cancer
For now the river is a rusted wheelchair
& a syringe & a bloody pig's hoof
& a boy shuffling cards with porn stars on them

And unto the people answered thus Festus:

Sons of Africville, of Antigonish, of Wolfville!
Wolf children of Bear River, bear children of Sackville!
Saccharine sons of Lunenburg, bear witness!
Shaggy sons shagging loons in Shag Harbour!

O virgins of the Bedford Basin!

I shall be all the families of the Maritimes,
& you shall be my people

Arise & let us go to the Commons
Arise & let us follow the river

where it winds across the palm of your hand

Holy Cross Cemetery

Electricity makes the Bone Ghost fizz
like fairy floss on the tongue; he hums distractedly,
sploshing in fengrass. Look, his footprints
spark & spit & (see!) he swags like a hurt bird.

>   Edmund Fultz
>   Died July 21, 1899
>   Aged 58 Years

Surprised by a power line he swoons, hands
on knees, spits a red vine. "See?!" he wags
the Deaf Man's map, smeared by his own paw
seeping.

>   And His Wife
>   Catherine Druhan
>   Died 1926

His TV hand trembles in front of
South Park St.—on screen, all's placid (an oak,
rubyyellow leaves, grey stones, SUVs,
the Orwellian infirmary) when suddenly the river

>   R.I.P.

floods the living road, a luminous wall
gouging course
over the matchstick City to the Atlantic
this brown vein of a god.

Festus Maximus, To Himself

A sky unlike. Afternoon creeps.
Where'd the Bone Ghost go?
(Likely pedalling my bike out of Hellifax!)

A pigeon *sotto voce*, a park bench,
—I, dragging on a perfecto,

have had to learn the simplest things
last. Slow in school, in love,
to find questions.
                    Parapraxis, the mouth
concrete. Once, on this spot, a boy struck me
so hard the street spun. I crawled
bawling through a cabal of schoolgirls.

Have learned
you islands
of women & boys
backwards.

This City stretches from my feet.

Off-Course, Citadel Hill, the Bone Ghost Sings of Electricity

Under power cables he masticates a-carolling

Video, boy! Audio, stereo, the Marconi Radio!

Bytes o' memory, call display, a battery: double A!

Datagram, telegram, cablegram, TV cable man!

Telegraph, teletype, typewriter, amplitude modulator!

Megaphone! Dictaphone, payphone, iPhone!

Map Song N° 1

I was an axe
cut for the small
hand of Ta'pit.
After dinner
he would hurl me
into an ash tree.
In dusk light
the tree scowled,
cheeks scarred,
sunken. I was
stolen & buried.

The White Well, 1861

Sailors disgorge from grog shops
on Knock 'em down Street,
hurl a bottle at a horse,
sing a ring around a whore
(drop of venom
on her tongue)
    as Septemus Hawkins,
the negro constable giant—
in his flea-bitten army finery,
bloodspattered sash, broadsword,
epaulets, cap backwards,
& one long feather!
steps as if out of a dream
wearing a mob of boys
like a pestilent wedding dress
—drags *another negro*,
a cutpurse, to the whipping post
for thirty-nine lashes
with a cat-o'-nine-tails
    as Presbyterian matrons
tow buckets of laundry
to the White Well
—now a manhole
on Brunswick
   from which the Bone Ghost
evading nonparticulate radiation
emerges, TV hand spitting

*Sailor boy Festus & a tall girl
picnic on a blanket by a brook,
sunshine, she in floral dress
pours maple syrup, Festus winks
through a hole in his pancake*

The Girding of Spring Garden Road

So cried the fouleyed Bone Ghost—
"When God intends to lay waste a City
he inspires violence in a wicked citizen.
Thereto gird thyself for any vagaries of *vox populi*."

        F.: "But—"
              (On the TV hand—
Vagary 1. Festus girds himself with cyclopean hos trolling the library
Vagary 2. With the moonbull of the liquor store, Festus girds himself
Vagary 3. Festus girds himself with the fat of mighty capitalistas in Cadillacs
Vagary 4. He girds himself with the Sisters of Charity cantillating
    O Wound of Festus
Vagary 5. He girds himself with shadows broken loose from under the skirt
    of the Bride of Dalhousie who yawps *Womb oh womb o river*
    coursing through ductus deferens of water coursing omphalos of
    Nile Jordan Seine oh! & when she succeeds in conjuring it,
    it drowns her)

"Which citizen?" asks Festus.
                Laughs the Bone Ghost: "You're all *I* see."

F.: (wrapped altogether in his wound
—to the City, which has edged up
near enough to hear him): "I am not the one you're looking for … "

Park Lane Mall, An Introduction

I.

Bone Ghost falters under the great awning
of Dairy Queen
in sight of Park Lane the magnificent

(1000 rhapsodic shoppers in its bowels—
when they breathe
they breathe they breathe
it sighs). Festus scoops the fiend
like a sack of rats' teeth,

crosses the thoroughfare,
kicks open glass doors,
lays him beside a mall map,
turns away
elated under strip lights.

The Bone Ghost drowns
on electrostatic fields, narratives.
A brood of bargain hunters
warm their furs by
the combusting apparition.

II.

Pad pad, O Fop, sneering at uncoifed shoppers,
deplorable dressers! Yes, roll your eyes
at this guard who has submitted to gloom.
Why, Fop, do *you* who would not offer
a sip of bottled water to a dying god
feel a sudden urge to take off your hat,
lower your head, get down on your knees
—for *them!*—your secret body revealed,
everywhere unprotected? Snigger,
yes, shake it off, wipe nose on a kerchief
by an escalator groaning like an iceberg.
How it turns. A third turning of the wheel,
your hard in-breath, *Om Mani Padme
hrrrrr*—you mistake the gyres of fate
thundering for … (I see your end: *Smack!*
the boom against your head, at sea
with your son, your manicured nails
pawing dark waves)—Ho! such a one.
As you pass, this row of manikins
seems to bow.

Festus Engages Spring Garden Road in Dialogue

Festus:

Park Lane: Rivers make energy;
      energy makes the escalator turn.

Hermit Crab at Park Lane Aquarium

     How much!
eddying upon
  this current, unseen
    river, gilded
alchemy
  tumbling,
    O Catherine
Druhan,
  whithersoever
    thou wentest
—& her husband,
  primordials
    long gone
from our plastic antechambers—
  sepulchres
    of memory
where I'll sleep
  with my fathers,
    such *creatures*—
How much!
  This hermit crab
    drags his theatre
in a polystyrene shipwreck,
  imagining
    it's the ocean …
In the glass—
  I, Festus,
    son of Gilgamesh,
having just slain
  an ogre
    halfway through

my shopping trip—
    my reflection,
        eyes half-
mast, mouth
    a shark
        laid to waste
on a ship's deck
    (& behind my face!
        adults at desks
stare at me,
    bored as demons
        at Xmas—
Was I a *teacher?*
    But of *what*
        to *whom?*)
The sound of water
    flushing
        & electricity—
corporeal memory:
    —judgments
        best forgotten.

Map, in Electric Light

shimmering map held against boggle-eyed phosphorescent shoppers
reveals a mallway of bright red throbbing fruit on a single tree
cash or credit no matter rejoice in the extinction of the enemy
whose face of a girl behind the map makes (o makes) the boy's apple
fall *bonk* off the branch

Down

No, I don't remember you,
stutters Festus
to the tall girl.

She smiles, leads him
to elevators of glass
they take up-down
laughing down-up
waving at the guard
in his booth
below.

Takes his hand
and *he trusts her.*

At the candy store
a hatchet-faced clerk leans
over the counter,
puts an orange candy band
on the girl's ring finger,
& on Festus' too,
 pronouncing:
 To keep in good stead
 beyond the City gates …

Riding the escalator
down, she puts Festus' ring
finger & all
in her mouth,
watches him,
 her eyes bottle-green, sharp;

long dark mane of hair
greying but she so young!
So tall, clumsy—

he too presses
his lips to each
of her fingertips
        & she leads him
        further, further
            down,
            paying his admission

    down

    into the
    cinemas

where they open their eyes—

    Audience (as one): Be warned!
        This will not be any easier
        with the lights out!
            Open, curtains.

Open Curtains

I.

Dark.
In the front row Girl & Festus
find two seats.

Air,
full house deep under the street,
colon of the Mall.

Audience:
In you, O Festus, have we taken refuge!
In you, Festus, the horns of righteousness shall be honked!
To you, Festus, have we given our hands!
From you, Festus, we expect a gentle answer!
With you we shall be delivered from the hunter's hand!
From woe, O Festus, in this dread City
That crawls at the door of the sea,
From the rattle of plasma TVs, noise of the whip!

Festus (to audience):
Shhhhhhhhh … The movie's starting!

> *On screen—*
> > *Festus rides*
> > *his Bicycle,*
> > *a Girl on back,*
> > *yellow leaves*
> > *of November,*
> > *she in the blue*

wool sweater
he gave her

(—Christmas Eve!
They sit on the floor
awaiting midnight,
a pile of gifts
between them
wrapped in newspaper)

holding him tight
over his leather jacket

he crosses Robie Street,
she shuts her eyes,
leaves swirl
around her feet

Audience:
Do ye recognize her, Festus?
Ah, ye two ships, ye two ships!
Look now! *Look!*

Festus:
Oh, Sally!
My Sally!

II.

Audience:
Fess up, Sally! What art thou to him?
In this Calvary of haddock, of scallop,
of trout! This Bayt Lahm of cod,
of salmon, of clam! What art thou,
in the consecrated seat beside our Festus!
Mother or matricide?
Mistress or exterminator?
Angel or debutante?

Sally:
Denizens, none of these!
I am the lake-swimmer!
The cross-stitcher! The novel-reader!
The potato chip-eater!
The angry, thrashing lover!
The small-cat-admirer!
Wearer of dresses with flower patterns!
I am his first true love!

Audience:
Oh! The Bride of Festus!

Festus:
Quiet! A good part!

On screen—
> *Festus wakes in bed
> with a big yawn & smile:*
> "*Good morning, Sally!
> Good morning to you, Mr. Sun!
> Good morning, bedroom!
> Good morning, neighbours!
> Morning, hookers! Morning, Halifax!
> Morning great fat Hali seals!
> Morning, sea! Come!
> Let us drink our fill of love all day long!*"

Audience:
Betrayer, charmer, trickster, *whoa!*
Ludic Man—
Behold, the lake-swimmer!
The cross-stitcher! Novel-reader!
Behold the small-cat-admirer!
Wearer of dresses with flower patterns!
Ahead, yo! This ship drifting toward you, still.
Behold your Bride!
Or have you forgotten, Festus?

Map (from inside his pocket):
Remember your way, Festus.
The path of the benevolent Deaf Man.

Festus: Stones moan, the Deaf Man went deaf.
Audience: The veins of Festus are fusion cables!
Festus: Cloudburst of blood, the Deaf Man swam to Bordeaux.

Audience: Festus searches out Freshwater River!
Festus: The Deaf Man gored toreadors with ink.
Audience: The heart of Festus is a local area network!
Festus: The Deaf Man fingernailed the devil to the wall.
Audience: To Festus, plastic is stone. This Mall, Stonehenge!

The hero can almost hear
a gushing
under the cinema.

III.

Festus: Were you my Bride?
Sally: You don't remember?
Festus: No, nothing.
Sally: General in particulars.
Festus: Till death do?
Sally: Beyond remonstrance.
Festus: "The good times."
Sally: The Sylvia Hotel.
Festus: Our house!
Sally: Restrained angles & lines.
Festus: Your small eyes.
Sally: You weren't the same.
Festus: You weren't curious.
Sally: You vanished!

Audience:
By the blood of the slain, Festus, *why did you vanish?*

On screen (a chewing sound)—
Sally carries a candle
through a dark apartment,
step by step, face lit
with flame, past a baleful
painting of her sister,
past a calico cat
whose eyes follow her,
past their shared bed,
stove, fridge, couch,
to a dark corner
where Festus crouches
tearing out & eating
page after page
of his prized comic,
Tales of Suspense #39

Sally:
O Halifax, Halifax! Festus vanished!
Out of his own name,
like a dying soldier
crawling out of his armour.

Audience:
Our Festus!
You tried to vanish out of *Festus*?

Festus:
My name was burning!

Audience:
Your name was drifting the narrows
packed with picric acid
toward another ship!
Starboard! Starboard!—All overboard!
Remember?

Festus:
Memory is a man on fire,
blurred by the warp of heat.
Memory the fire itself
and the man *and* his final thoughts.

Audience:
By the memory of Freshwater River, Sally—
why did *you* vanish?

> *On screen—*
>> *Union Station, Sally leans*
>> *out the door of a train,*
>> *at her feet a box, two cats*
>> *—one calico, one black—*
>> *skirling, Sally's sister*
>> *holds her, Festus stares,*
>> *sailors march between,*
>> *letters flicker on the board*

Sally:
The City was in flames.

Audience:
Then how, Bride of Festus, do we live?

Sally:
All in flames.

IV.

Audience:
If this be true, O Festus, tell us the story of the earth!

Festus:
Oh, shut *up*, why don't you!

> *On screen—*
>> *Sally stuffs objects into a bag:*
>> *a framed portrait of La Anima Sola;*
>> *a wallet, fat with photos*
>> *& cards & notes; a stack*
>> *of books; a Swiss Army Knife.*
>> *Festus, in a window, watches her*
>> *burrow in the dirt*
>> *with her bare hands.*
>> *She drops the bag in the hole,*
>> *jabs the knife into a tree*
>> *with all her strength,*
>> *& walks upstairs to make dinner.*
>> *Festus tiptoes down,*
>> *pulls out the knife.*

> *In his hands it changes*
> *into his heart.*
> *He lowers it into the hole.*

Audience:
(mixed booing & applause)

> *On screen—*
> > *Festus, holding a knife*
> > *caked with dirt,*
> > *watches a train drift away …*

V.

Audience:
Awake, Festus,
in these chambers of death!
Citizen in the City of yourself.
With fire, render hearts oblivious!
With freezing rainwater, render hands numb!
With squalls, render ears dumb!
With earthquakes, render eyes dim!
Awake!

> *On screen—*
> > *One foggy morning, Halifax harbour,*
> > *hung over, World War I,*
> > *hundreds of grey tanks on the water,*
> > *logs in formation, pirate ships,*
> > *songs uprising, Yo, ho! Yo, ho … !*

*At the narrows two ships
skip off each other, breaking a tooth,
a broadaxe, sparking, the male
aflame! spitting mad, the female
awake with munitions,
aflame! after a long night,
you know the kind, such a long night,
Haligonians milling on piers
to watch—Look! Oh, look ... 9:06.
The harbour inhales deeply
& exhales   all,   all!*

      The
           glass sky
                      s—h—a—t—t—e—r—s!

A shower of popcorn kernels ...
Far under the street,
a deluge
of white light!

Map:
O!

From Sally's seat
          to the exit
                   a blazing trail—
Festus, smouldering,
candy ring aflame, shards of glass in his eyes,
hurt blind.

Sally Gone

Festus stumbles into sunlight.

Scratches head.
No, nothing comes back,
nothing
       of shadows witnessed.
Something, though,
is *gone*, & this wound
on his hand leaks
droplets of orange sugar
on the sidewalk
trailing west
toward the Public Gardens
where he *runs*.

Et tu, alien Mall.
Why do you arch two manicured-
rows-of-fir-tree eyebrows
                    toward him?

Public Gardens, 1761

Farrago. Warm postmeridian of swans, weddings,
a swineherd or two sunning,

Halifax hoi polloi byke round a civil fête
of ragtag pioneers, Injuns ("Dawnger! Dawnger!"

shrieks Gen. E. Massey, behind a widow)
& footsore Festus

in paper pirate hat, sipping a Dixie cup
of mulled wine, rubs eyes

with fetid ringfinger
bandaged throbbing *O Sally!*—as

Abbé Maillard, preambling daintily, gloves swirling,
decodes a rattlebrained scroll

for Mi'kmaq chief Jeannot Peguidalonet
who, belching, drops hatchet in hole.

All present in view of God's river drink the King's health
Hoo-rah!

Byplay

Park Lane hauls glass torso
into vaulted sky
balances on two ponderous parkades

Rejoice! ye false prophets
wagging signs
that *HE WILL COME*

Behold! shop doors
bleed
glass slippers

Woe, harlots, fools!
lifting skirts over heads
to reveal your nakedness
to the vernix'd god

It lists, as if listening,
still as a fridge
with morphine
in the icebox

& lets rip
a Godzilla-at-Coney-Island roar.

By-Ground Sally

Long shadow of an empty gazebo
uncurls over Festus, heart hatchet-heavy,
kicking stones.
   A Feral Girl—
blur of grey hair & bare force,
breasts vast & dangling,
pubic hair bursting
—burrows with a compact mirror
into the scarred mound
where Peguidalonet planted the axe,
fistfuls of lakefront flung
over her shoulder.

Festus sniffs her—
tackles & pins her on grass, bites her mouth

("No!")
  & tastes
    & tastes her.

Oxen, Sun

In a fog of sleep
beside Princess Sally,
the hero could
never have known

> *Sally behind frosted train glass*
> *crying printer's ink ...*
>
> *"Where's my heroine?" (slurs he)*
> *"Relax, relax—" (chugs*
>
> *the engine). Her door floating off*
> *propelled by a bike chain gobbed with tar & coal,*
>
> *her scent of*
>   *"—go to a flick or something," she waves*

a cracked axe, from a hole at her feet.

He opens his eyes—Sally drifts off with it.

Map Song N° 2

I was a faded tattoo
on the shoulder
of a sad drunk hipster
at the North End Diner—
of the goblin *Duende*
blowing his horn
in the anagogic night

Ceremony—Eating in Front of TV

Festus—(slumped
        in his armchair;

                past the curtains, a
                pigeon shattered in the sun)—

Memory: She held
you sobbing in bed till you trembled to a stop.

TV: (skyblue light) But I promise
        that won't happen to you again.

What Park Lane Thinks, Stomping Public Gardens

Bright sun, control button, memory button, power button.
Encryption.

Surveillance camera, grass piazza, digital data.
Electronica, a Toyota.

Analogue phone line, digital. A pixelated billboard, a baby crying.

Optical scanner. Hacker. Escalator, elevator,
automatic sliding door.

Swan, search engine. Ghostbox, dead wing.
Blank screen.

Bar code, brake cord, up- or download.
Pond.

Motion detector, transmitter.
Sunflower.

Wire. The
gates.

In Memoriam, Sally

Park Lane, proud wedding guest,
                hair in high mists

   (Taller by far
   than the Aliant Building, that sad seawitness:
   O foolish rectitude!
   O wretched faithfulness!)

stomps RAM!
after li'l stumblin' Festus into the Gardens
both of them sniffin' the river source
RAM! the fundament quakes
Hello! the Aliant Building RAM! *fell'd!*
Of all things! horrendous Fenwick Tower
RAM! *fell'd! Can it be!*
the grain elevators too
all tumbling RAM! like concrete kites

& Sally—
axe in hand upon the sidewalk, blood trembling
like wine in a bottle
            under an anvil

III. THE COW

Festus, Hansel & Grendel

I.

Live music
from a storm window

What gardens, these?
What Victorian mansions?

Past a memory
of Saint Paul dying
in John Doull's Bookstore

What City is this what street river square?
What plan?

A seagull gorges on a starfish
beside the casino funhouse
arching its mouth
its neck full
of chronicles
of harbour

idiotic laughter drifts
from inside

Lo, the Citadel a skull,
a ship carrying us
inland
away from dreams

us beggars
us Lebanese falafel vendors
us charlatans
us strung-out mothers
us parricides

treading lightly
where once were landmines
hearing the steady heart-
beat of the good Town Clock
east side of our hill
Golgotha of the Maritimes

I stand
at the City's highest point
locked out

II.

Then came all the troglodyte tribes of Supernova Scotia
to festoon'd Festus, digressive descendent
o' George Dunk (videlicet, *Lord Halifax*,
sponsor to Edward Cornwallis,
1749)
  —spake they,
    "Behold, O Festus,
we *are* thy bone & thy flesh!"

"Nay!" saith Festus mallslayer.
"My bone & flesh are *memory.*"

The populous howled:
"In this apogee of the age of Festus
have we taken refuge in *you*,
our captain, as streams of water
gushed from the sun & moon,
as Park Lane married a streetlight,
fertilizing the void with kinescopic sight,
as inconceivable tattoos unfolded
in the sky over Bayer's Lake. Now,
again, lead us across this fog of memory!
Protect us & help us & feed us!
Where have the cows gone, *our* cattle
that once grazed on Citadel Hill?"

Festus bullshithater
made this answer—

Zealots, I am as scared as you, blown
    by the wind of the poem
        to the backside of a river,
cowboy
    on the night
        of a new constellation
—so familiar
but I don't know what it means.
            When, zealots,
you set out on my journey, a caveat:
your heart is an amulet you carry
through the forest of memory.
Hold the amulet to your naked chest
or the trees will show themselves to be devils

& the owls on their branches
will speak your dossier to them.

Do not trade your amulet for gold
or love or hamburgers. Close your eyes—
see how it glitters?

Were There Testimonials?

Byland, dinnertime, 1860. Streets of white pine
overgrown. Cattlerun, cascade

of pioneer kine from Citadel Hill to the river
south across an intervale of swamp.

A fiefdom.
Festus kneels on pine needles, unfolds map

of his bike, sighs
beside a pond: viz., *Up-kuch-coom-mouch way-gad-die.*

Old Ben Morris, a Mi'kmaq,
milk planets for eyes, raising from a deadfall

a dripping fur.

Map Song N° 3

I was a cow
lowing on the hill
above the town
as Henrietta
a shipwright's wife
charwoman
fingers defeated
hair ash
ground her
teeth to sparks

The Egg Pond

Froths, freezes. Mizzle. Victorian toughs on skates
steer wenches in corsets.
F. reads map, steps north—

ice browns into wet toast. Cows plod hoofhigh
in fenland. Drakes.
F. reads map, steps north—

desiccation, a cement eggshell,
duckless. A Pubescent Girl
with huge glasses, on a swing, shivers,

grins. Young thugs yowl,
Where ya get that see-gar you too young t' smoke!
F. panics, steps

north upon a skateboard & bicycle bowl
circumnavigated by such electrical wonderment
no ghost survives.

Park Lane Approacheth

If as they say Calypso does not reside on McNabs Island
& I am not the hero

why do I hear footsteps?

Humungous Bos Taurus!

                Heads up, F.!
Through the Wanderers Grounds
lumbers a hundred foot cow. That's right, I said
a hundred foot cow! It
doesn't mean you any harm
yet toward you it plods,
                gaining force.
                          In fact
as we speak it turns into a steam engine,
skyhigh!
      Pistons: *suck-a-suck!*
                      Valves: *ptweet-ptweet!*
Past the Museum of Natural History
toward you, agape by the Egg Pond,
it clacks
      more like a a jalopy, now—
So big, the frame! So loud, the wheezing!
Upon thin wheels
it stutters it backfires
           now at last
revealing itself: Park Lane Mall! all brutalist
concrete, tinted glass
           but now (*holy
cow!*) itself once more,
incubus capacious crayfish ascurryin' toward ye
                        clickers up!

Bullfight

Eye of
Commons

where cows grazed
crows gaze

fountain gushes
rainbows

a wrinkled medicine man
palms his eyes

smells a calf
gashed gored grilled

gift wrapped
for Gen. E. Massey

at Wendy's
down the block

Showdown with Park Lane the Crayfish

Ancient decapod scurries
onto Commons, cuts an infield apart
with escalator-sharp pleopods.
Mandibles chew a lamppost to paste.

Wee Festus dives for cover.
Shoppers cascading from abdominal plates
are milled by the dangling
front claws.

Oh glorious Crustacea!
Hoist thy tanklike carapace upon
our fountain hub (Whoa!
Thud.

Ceremony—Diving into a Good Movie

          Ouch!
The glass crayfish squats
where paths meet
like spokes of a whorl,
the beast *dead still*
        first time in history.

Twilight.
Festus circles its antennae;
no kids
but a big dog barks.

Water gushes from double doors.

He asks the coiled sky for mercy.
Horses of the sun bear down
on the City. *Mercy*, he repeats.
He breathes.
Before hearing a response
              he dives between fanged shards
into the foyer
    where water
    stands.

In the promenade,
        he floats past the guard booth
among precious things:
        fiddle!
           comic!
              star-

   fish!
     cow!
       sign (*Clearance Sale Now!*)
            a robin, so small, red-
            sopped, wrong-
            side up …

Ho, a sailor! *Hail ye fellow.*
    Well met, well met!

In wineclear brine
matching current, heart
downsunk
fathoms under Halifax
again! pit-
a-pat, body
drifting
   to Empire Cinemas,
   empty
   seat.

   Blank

   screen.

Festus, The Movie

F., scarf billowing, gazes at waves. A cat pontificates.

Deaf chap hands him a map. They spit in palms, clasp hands.

Duel with a Bone Ghost. Misreckonings.

Victory. Bone Ghost renders seraphic river map.

Sacrifice of Sally at food court. Watch fractured, 9:06.

Hero swings princess to safety by transmission cable!

(Festus, riveted
to seat, from a popcorn bag a vine
winds his larynx, from speakers & projector
ivy luxuriance blossoms
to gloriole, a crown about his head;
on screen Park Lane reels,
staggers, thighs of plastic, glass—
power lines pullulate,
TVs depict stars dying, effigies)

Boy carried off on celestial wheels.

What Manner of Film Was This?

Light opens the cinema, *an eye*, soft
crimson chairs, sepia walls,
his stomach burns

Couples coo about where they have been in the dark
& Festus roars
    aloud, roars
       for loneliness
       in this light

A Maenad in the lobby
hat barely concealing horns
brooms flakes of popcorn
asks a question
    Festus does not hear
so he answers:

I have not put my confidence in gold.

She repeats
What film did you see?

It was, at that, on the birth of a warrior
named …

He shakes his head, nibbles a kernel,
glides up escalator, passes
food court, candy store,
aquarium,
    north up Spring Garden

past the Gardens—
day pools back of the skull
like bogwater.

Breathe deeply, Festus,
as if there were, you *knew*, out there
an existence beyond your own
which you damn near forgot.

You are walking on a vein.

What Lay at the Poem's Feet

And traverse, dear fettered one, the frozen forest,
under greyest cinderblock tenements & pastel storm porches
like trains steaming away, by maple trees
with sneakers & toilet paper wound in their hair
as braids of ash,
    City of ice! Pianos thump
songs of lost love—all that will be resurrected—
in the basements of the meek.

At the Commons fountain, under the moon,
a Little Girl,
    a resplendent bicycle.

Matronymics of the Girl

My word! This Girl of variable hue
—now dark black loam,
              now cerulean,
                            now peach—
pigtails, overalls,
thick eyebrows, wolfish eyes,
beside *his bike*:
              unlocked on the grass.

That's my bike!
says Festus.

The Girl
blocks his way, asks—

Do you hear, faintly, your word?

He shrugs, she signals
with a small finger
his pocket. He remembers
the map! But feels only
a soggy Kleenex
that crumbles in his hand.

She waits.
        His finger pokes a kernel
which he offers.
She places it on her tongue.
Nibbles.
Smiles.

Steps aside.

Showdown

Last iamb of light.

Asks Festus, *What is your name?*

She clears throat; the earth under him
trembles. The Commons trembles.
The word *sky*
trembles. She opens her mouth,
answers
        & Festus hears ... *River.*

She
is answering. She!

    Her fluvial voice
    gushing
    under the sky; her body's
    ancient water-
    course, this Girl
        the river!
            secret of the land
            in her small
            beaded purse.

And Festus sees trembling under the mute sky
    the ancient crayfish flipp'd, exoskeleton ajar
Sees the technology of the past & of the City itself expos'd
    grinding like innards of a pocket watch
Sees Bastard Time the capsiz'd dragon & holds its gaze
Sees Sally's legs sticking out from under the crayfish
    in her striped stockings & ruby slippers

Under the protean sky raining fire Festus sees myriads
    of sleeping Haligonians shimmering
    like bright red throbbing apples on a single tree
    hovering on the branch of City
Under an honest sky Festus sees Haligonians fleeing a great fire
    on burning wooden sidewalks stampeding before rows
    of burning shops leaping off the Kissing Bridge!
Festus sees the tongue of harbour curl'd shut the throat of peninsula
    curl'd shut the torso of City pool'd with blood
Watches denizens dream of drowning in narrow channels
    of the heart, each heart a wound,
    nerves winding through fork'd & veiny boughs
Festus hears the sky's articulations, dice flung by gods
    & his own heart the ancestral wood aflame
Sees past & future the same dense forest of sleeping bodies
    in the purple night under the hunchback moon
    a blur of bodies like propellers of a helicopter
Festus weeping sees the propellers slow down & slow down
    & can discern one body from another
And weeping he sees the crayfish vanish & the tree vanish
    & the river itself that rose after 100 years vanish
And sees the multitudes of gods that never vanish'd
    the orgy of gods in the forest of time
Festus sees Festus the City a god of many bodies
Festus sees each & every god & from the viewpoint of each god
    sees himself

        And the river *roars*—

Festus amnesiac, pourer of concrete, floored, remembers.
    Remembers!

    All, *all*.

Where You Been? Asks the River

                    Saith Festus:
I am nothing, shell, snail un-
curling to peninsula, to wolvessongs.

I, unblinking, awestruck,
raise & raze a bridge.
                    Oh, river!
I veil you with concrete, & forget.

—Forgot! And woke, citizen
in the City of Halifax. City of myself.

Little Girl (limpid):
I won't let that happen to you again.

He rolls the bike to her & helps her on
whispering, *1970 Schwinn Lemon Peeler* ...

She rides it away
up Welsford Street
& waves,
        waves!
                  gliding toward the Superstore.

He lives just one block farther, on Moran Street.
He'd been so close.

*My keys, by moonlight,
in my pocket all along.*

Festus walks home.

Acknowledgements

Many texts have contributed to—and, in some cases, have been robbed for—these poems. The books that were always within reach included Judith Fingard's *The Dark Side of Life in Victorian Halifax*, and *Halifax: The First 250 Years*; Thomas H. Raddall's *Halifax, Warden of the North*; *Canadian History: Confederation to the present*, edited by Martin Brook Taylor and Doug Owram; William Coates Borrett's *Tales Told Under the Old Town Clock*; Stephen A. Davis' *Mi'kmaq: People of the Maritimes*; and Janet F. Kitz's *Shattered City: The Halifax Explosion and the Road to Recovery*. Versions of the poems in *Festus* appeared in *Grain*, *The Fiddlehead*, *The Literary Review of Canada*, *Concrete News*, and *To Find Us: Words and Images of Halifax* (anthology): acknowledgment is made to the editors of these publications. My gratitude to the Nova Scotia Department of Tourism, Culture and Heritage, for assistance during a crucial stage in the development of the book. And to the Nova Scotia Archives. These were my teachers: Tonja Gunvaldsen Klaassen, Cory Lavender, Stephanie Yorke, Myka Tucker-Abramson, Emily Holton, Robyn Sarah, Blair Reeve, Sun Man Ho, and Jean Barger. At the 2006 Banff Writing Studio, Tim Bowling and Anne Simpson; and in particular Don McKay and Erina Harris, for getting excited about "the Halifax book." Nagoos Yovan Nagwetch, for corresponding with me about his *L'nu*, the Mi'kmaq. Aimee Parent Dunn and Dawn Kresan, for Palimpsest Press. Jim Johnstone, my editor, for the samurai dexterity of his cuts. And Tiina, for her ferocious patience and her love. Warm thanks.

Author Biography

John Wall Barger's poems have appeared in many journals and anthologies, including *The Cincinnati Review*, *Subtropics*, *The Malahat Review*, *Best Canadian Poetry* and The Montreal Prize *Global Poetry Anthology*. His earlier books include *Pain-proof Men* and *Hummingbird*: the latter was a finalist for the Raymond Souster Award.